THIS BOOK BELONGS TO

_____

13-Digit ISBN: 978-1-60433-840-9
10-Digit ISBN: 1-60433-840-7

This book may be ordered by mail from the publisher. Please include $5.99 for postage and handling. Please support your local bookseller first!

Books published by Cider Mill Press Book Publishers are available at special discounts for bulk purchases in the United States by corporations, institutions, and other organizations. For more information, please contact the publisher.

Cider Mill Press Book Publishers
"Where good books are ready for press"
12 Spring Street | PO Box 454
Kennebunkport, Maine 04046
Visit us on the Web! www.cidermillpress.com

The map on the cover of this notebook was originally printed in 1983 and is included for historical reference only. Please do not use the cover image for navigational purposes when exploring Acadia National Park.

Typography: Georgia, Hoefler Text, and Voluta Script Pro
Image Credits: All images used under official license from Shutterstock.com.
Printed in China
1 2 3 4 5 6 7 8 9 0
First Edition

ACADIA NATIONAL PARK

SIGNATURE EDITION

BOOK PUBLISHERS
KENNEBUNKPORT, MAINE

Introduction

There's a spirit here. On some level there's no other way to say it; you feel it the minute you round the corner along Ocean Drive and see the white stretch of Sand Beach nested in a rocky cove below you and the giants' steps of Otter Cliffs ahead of you, ascending from the Atlantic. You feel it when you climb past the first evergreen tops and are suddenly above the traffic and errands and back into the world you knew was here as a child, and has been—a world of mountains falling into gorges, and islands sprouting like tufts of moss in the distance of the ocean. It isn't just the drama of Acadia—the awe one feels at the foot of Denali or the rim of the Grand Canyon—it's something deeper, or closer, something *intimate* about the land—something that is ultimately approachable; perhaps it's a sense of the great age of this well-worn landscape, or of a violent power slowly smoothed into an awesome gentleness. Whatever it is, it becomes a part of us the moment we come in contact with it, like water drawn into salt.

Four hundred and twenty million years ago, two continental shelves collided, forming a line of volcanoes that was lifted and tilted by more collisions, carved for millions of years by erosion and then, in the last hundred thousand years, by glaciers as thick as a mile flowing over it, excavating lakes and rounding the rock once thrown up from the earth's mantle. The region formed by this process is now the coast of Downeast Maine, and the most dramatic of its features is a formation of rock once miles deep in a single caldera, still the highest peak along the eastern seaboard from Rio de Janeiro to Newfoundland, a row of long mountains rising directly from the ocean like something heaving itself up through the landscape. The name we know the park by today was inspired by the Greek region of Arcadia, long thought of as a refuge, or "rustic paradise." After Samuel de Champlain mapped *L'Isle des Monts Déserts* in 1604, his descriptions of this unique place were sufficient to convince French nobility to establish a Jesuit colony on the island just eight years later—a considerable honor, as it was the first of its kind in all of North America, in what they hoped would be New France, an area they called, *"Acadie."* As it happens, the Mi'kmaqs, who spent their summers here, used the suffix -*akadie* for "a place of abundance." The proximity in meaning of the French and the Native American names for this place is a testament to just how many people and peoples have been reminded of paradise by Mount Desert Island.

There is a spirit here. For two hundred years now artists, writers, and philosophers have come to share the truth, as they see it, about this place; one of my favorite results of this is Frederick Church's 1841 painting of Cadillac and Dorr as seen from Otter Cove, how the tiny settlers' homesteads in the fields show mankind's husbandry of nature while the mountains swell the frame of the image, two great and muscular beings leaned into each other, living in the sky.

Another testament to that spirit is Acadia's almost singular history of philanthropy and conservation. In 1901, a group of Harvard students founded a trust to purchase and protect the land for free public use, one of the first of its kind; these lands later formed the core of what became Acadia National Park. George Dorr gave his life and his fortune to adding to this preservation, developing the land for public recreation, and working tirelessly to get this nascent parcel protected under the aegis of the National Park Service. John D. Rockefeller Jr., in concert with some of the greatest talents in engineering and landscape architecture such as Frederick Law Olmsted Jr. and Beatrix Farrand, acquired a large parcel and developed a system of gardens and carriage roads, most of which he later endowed to the National Park. Today, the Friends of Acadia, well funded by myriad donors and literally thousands of volunteers, helps the Park acquire land, negotiate protective measures, and provide adequate stewardship for this singular place.

Otter Cove, now traversed by a sweeping road of laid stone arches, otherwise looks nearly the same today as it does in Church's painting: a smattering of houses in fields at the feet of those mountains still robed in their natural wilderness. In fact, I was through there just yesterday, a chilly and clear day in late October, with three colleagues, on my way from planning one trail project to the next. We were trying to figure out how to accommodate more than a thousand hikers a day on trails that were conceived in a time when there were dozens; how to keep the feel of a rugged hike in the woods while providing, simply, enough *room* for everyone who wants to be here.

When I was asked to be Poet Laureate of Acadia, my greatest anxiety in accepting that position was that I would need to write an occasional poem on the centennial of the Park. How, I worried, could I honor the deep commitment and life-giving venture of its founders while at the same time acknowledging the predicament that this place is in—not just because of how much we love to visit it, but because of what we, on the largest scale, are doing to the earth? Eventually I found my footing in the words of another poet, W.H.

Auden: "May I, composed...of Eros and of dust, show an affirming flame." That is, after all, what the Park's founders did, in the midst of what must have seemed just as troubling times, witnessing the clear-cutting of old growth pines and hemlocks now gone forever, the furious burst of house and hotel construction intruding into the reaches of the wilderness, the rumbling onslaught of the new automobile: they showed an affirming flame, they preserved for us this Eden. My own poem begins, "May we not wreck this place." It is a simple entreaty but the task, as any Park manager or trail crew worker can tell you, is far from easy, and lies before all of us.

I remember well my first hike in Acadia, now thirty years ago. I had just started my job on the trail crew and my boss had dropped me off at the Beachcroft Path trailhead. I remember leaving the road, and the traffic noise fading behind me as I followed the hallway of the trail through hardwoods and sparse spruces, and how the trail became a continuous path of flat-laid stones edged by coping rocks sometimes as tall as my chest, set down a century ago. How I began to feel I had entered another world—a sort of world of the past, but a world in which what was true for the past is still true, will continue to be true. I remember following those steps as in a dream, each bend in the trail like opening an ancient gate, each sudden blue glimpse of Frenchman Bay like a revelation, as though someone had finally raised the blinds in a room I had been sitting in for years. How, at the top, teetering over the Atlantic, looking down into its field sown with islands, I knew where I belonged—that it might not be here, at Acadia, always, but that it was unquestionably here on this planet. I hadn't known that before, nor had I known that I didn't yet know it. That kind of awakening becomes possible here and, perhaps, is the most important thing one can say about Acadia. I hope you experience it, too. I hope it changes you, like one continental shelf colliding with another. I hope it serves as a sign of how Eden can persist. Big hopes indeed, but they seem perfectly natural when you are truly here.

Christian Barter was the Centennial Poet Laureate of Acadia National Park in 2016. For over twenty-five years he has worked for Acadia as a trail crew supervisor, stone worker, rigger, and arborist. He was a recipient of The Hodder Fellowship from Princeton University and is the author of three books of poetry including Bye-Bye Land, *winner of the 2017 Isabella Gardner Award. His poetry has appeared in journals and other media outlets such as* Ploughshares, The American Scholar, Tin House, The Writer's Almanac, Poetry Daily, *and* The PBS Newshour.

"An Act To establish the Lafayette National Park in the State of Maine," approved by Congress, formally rededicating Sieur de Monts National Monument, which would eventually become Acadia National Park (February 26, 1919).

whether for homestead, mineral, right of way, or any other purpose whatsoever, or shall affect the rights of any such claimant, locator, or entryman to the full use and enjoyment of his land and nothing herein contained shall affect, diminish, or impair the right and authority of the county of Coconino, in the State of Arizona, to levy **Bright Angel Toll Road and Trail. Purchase authorized.** and collect tolls for the passage of live stock over and upon the Bright Angel Toll Road and Trail, and the Secretary of the Interior is hereby authorized, to negotiate with the said county of Coconino for the purchase of said Bright Angel Toll Road and Trail and all rights therein, and report to Congress at as early a date as possible the terms upon which the property can be procured.

Rights of way authorized. Vol. 31, p. 790. Sec. 5. That whenever consistent with the primary purposes of said park the Act of February fifteenth, nineteen hundred and one, applicable to the locations of rights of way in certain national parks and the national forests for irrigation and other purposes, and subsequent Acts shall be and remain applicable to the lands included within the park. **For railroads.** The Secretary of the Interior may, in his discretion and upon such conditions as he may deem proper, grant easements or rights of way for railroads upon or across the park.

Mineral prospecting permitted. Sec. 6. That whenever consistent with the primary purposes of said park, the Secretary of the Interior is authorized, under general regulations to be prescribed by him, to permit the prospecting, development, and utilization of the mineral resources of said park upon such terms and for specified periods, or otherwise, as he may deem to be for the best interests of the United States.

Irrigation projects. Sec. 7. That, whenever consistent with the primary purposes of said park, the Secretary of the Interior is authorized to permit the utilization of areas therein which may be necessary for the development and maintenance of a Government reclamation project.

Building, etc., restrictions on private lands. Sec. 8. That where privately owned lands within the said park lie within three hundred feet of the rim of the Grand Canyon no building, tent, fence, or other structure shall be erected on the park lands lying between said privately owned lands and the rim.

Grand Canyon National Monument vacated. Sec. 9. The Executive order of January eleventh, nineteen hundred and eight, creating the Grand Canyon National Monument, is hereby revoked and repealed, and such parts of the Grand Canyon National **Park lands excluded from game preserve. Vol. 34, p. 607.** Game Preserve, designated under authority of the Act of Congress, approved June twenty-ninth, nineteen hundred and six, entitled "An Act for the protection of wild animals in the Grand Canyon Forest Reserve," as are by this Act included with the Grand Canyon National Park are hereby excluded and eliminated from said game preserve.

Approved, February 26, 1919.

February 26, 1919.
[S. 4957.]
[Public, No. 278.]

CHAP. 45.—An Act To establish the Lafayette National Park in the State of Maine.

Be it enacted by the Senate and House of Representatives of the United States of America in Congress assembled, That the tracts of land, ease- **Lafayette National Park, Me. Sieur de Monts National Monument changed to. Vol. 34, p. 295. Vol. 39, p. 1785.** ments, and other real estate heretofore known as the Sieur de Monts National Monument, situated on Mount Desert Island, in the county of Hancock and State of Maine, established and designated as a national monument under the Act of June eighth, nineteen hundred and six, entitled "An Act for the preservation of American antiquities," by presidential proclamation of July eighth, nineteen hundred and sixteen, is hereby declared to be a national park and dedicated as a public park for the benefit and enjoyment of the people under the name of the Lafayette National Park, under which name the aforesaid national park shall be entitled to receive and to use all

The parks do not belong to one state or to one section...

The Yosemite, the Yellowstone, the Grand Canyon are national properties in which

every citizen has a vested interest;

they belong as much to the man of Massachusetts, of Michigan, of Florida, as they do to the people of California, of Wyoming, and of Arizona.

—Stephen T. Mather, first National Park Service Director
(1917-1929)

Mount Desert Island was discovered in 1604 by Samuel Champlain, who named it, "L'Isle des Monts Déserts," meaning "island of barren mountains."

Acadia was first established as Sieur de Monts National Monument in July 1916 by President Woodrow Wilson; it was not until January 1929 that it was officially named Acadia National Park.

The name honors both the history of French settlement in the region and reaches even further back to the belief held by those settlers that this region was akin to Arcadia, a pristine wilderness in ancient Greece.

Otter Cliff at sunrise with fog and rough seas.

The park consists of 49,052 acres, including 30,300 acres on Mount Desert Island, 2,728 acres on Isle au Haut, and 2,366 acres on the Schoodic Peninsula.

∽

Average Weather Conditions:

Average Spring Temperature
30°F to 70°F (-1°C to 21°C)

Average Summer Temperature
Daytime: 45°F to 90°F (7°C to 32°C)
Ocean temperature: 50°F to 60°F
(10°C to 16°C)
Lake temperatures: 55°F to 70°F
(13°C to 21°C)

Average Fall Temperature
30°F to 70°F (-1°C to 21°C)

Average Winter Temperature
14°F to 35°F (-10°C to 2°C)

The breezes from the Atlantic, mingling with **the life-giving breath of the forest of pine and spruce, the matchless grandeur of the distant views, the beauty and picturesqueness of the immediate surroundings...** If ever nature indicated a beneficent purpose of affording health and enjoyment to the souls of men, she has done it on Mount Desert Island.

—Statement of the Honorable David B. Ogden before the subcommittee of the Committee of Public Lands House of Representatives 65th Congress, second session on H. R. 11935, A Bill to Establish the Mount Desert National Park in the State of Maine (May 30, 1918)

Sand Beach in winter.

Each breaking wave, each rush of the sea on the slope of sand, reminds me why these places of pilgrimage matter. They matter to me because in the long view, I do not.

I am driftwood.
I am rockweed.
I am osprey and the mackerel in the clutch of her feet.

I am a woman standing on the edge of the continent looking out.

—Terry Tempest Williams, *The Hour of Land: A Personal Topography of America's National Parks* (2016)

A barred owlet.

Afternoon in October.

Thunder Hole has earned its name from the cavernous sound created by waves forcing water into a small cave and crashing against the air in the cave; to hear the loudest claps of "thunder" visit between high and low tide.

God molded his world largely
and mightily off this marvelous
coast and meant that

in the tired days
of life men should
come and worship
here and renew
their spirit.

This I have done and turning
I go to work again.

—W. E. B. DuBois, from "Of Beauty and Death," published in
Darkwater: Voices from Within the Veil (1920)

Bass Harbor Head Light, the only lighthouse in Acadia, was established in 1858. The fourth-order Fresnel lens, manufactured in Paris, has been in use there since 1902.

Bass Harbor Head Light at sunset.

There are few spots, if any, which can combine the variety and luxuriance of the eastern forests in such small compass.

—Franklin K. Lane, Secretary of the Interior, before the subcommittee of the Committee of Public Lands House of Representatives 65th Congress, second session on H. R. 11935, A Bill to Establish the Mount Desert National Park in the State of Maine (May 30, 1918)

There are 26 mountains in the park. Cadillac Mountain, at 1,530 feet is the highest peak in Acadia (and the tallest mountain on the U.S. Atlantic coast), while Flying Mountain is the lowest at 284 feet.

❧

The Atlantic Ocean, as seen from Cadillac Mountain.

On clear mornings,
standing on this great whaleback of granite, with its coastal world at your feet,
you can see the roundness of the earth in your mind's eye and sense keenly the orderliness of the solar system, the way the sun and the moon pull on the oceans to the advantage of life on earth.

—Christopher Camuto, from *Time and Tide in Acadia:
Seasons on Mount Desert Island* (2009)

The forests are largely primeval.
Oaks, beeches, birches, maples, ashes,
poplars, and many other deciduous
trees of our eastern ranges,

here found in
full luxuriance,

mingle with groves of pine and
giant hemlock. The typical shrubs of
northeastern America are in equal
abundance. Wild flowers abound.

—Franklin K. Lane, Secretary of the Interior, before the
subcommittee of the Committee of Public Lands House of
Representatives 65th Congress, second session on H. R. 11935,
A Bill to Establish the Mount Desert National Park
in the State of Maine (May 30, 1918)

A scenic view from Ocean Path.

In less than half a century the Island, first regarded as merely a rocky, barren, and largely inhospitable wilderness, far distant from emerging metropolitan centers along the Eastern seaboard, became a scenic destination for thousands of Americans.

—Pamela Belanger, author of *Maine in America* (2000)

Acadia is home to more than 300 species of birds, making it one of the premier bird-watching areas in the country.

There are more than 50 species of mammals on land and at sea, including seals, dolphins, and whales.

The park is also home to 1,000 species of flowering plants.

Truth eventually reaches us like the crashing surf at Thunder Hole, the place in Acadia where unexpected waves can pull us into the sea.

—Terry Tempest Williams, *The Hour of Land: A Personal Topography of America's National Parks* (2016)

But now that I've moved away,
with each return it all becomes
almost hallucinatory:

the dark blue water,
the rocky coast with
occasional flashes
of white sand,

the jasper stone beaches along
the coast, the pine and fir forests
somehow vivid in their stillness.

—Alexander Chee, from "Acadia National Park: Maine's Bright Face"
(*The New York Times,* June 30, 2016)

View through the forest on the Wonderland Trail.

There are 26 lakes and ponds on Mount Desert Island; Jordan Pond, with a depth of 150 feet, is the deepest body of water in Acadia.

If fog comes, enjoy its gift: a softening of sights and sounds.

—"This Small Seaside National Park is One of the Most Visited"
(*National Geographic*, November 5, 2009)

Sunrise from Cadillac Mountain reveals a coastline carved with a crooked knife.

—Christopher Camuto, from *Time and Tide in Acadia: Seasons on Mount Desert Island* (2009)

Sunrise from the Summit of Cadillac Mountain in fall.

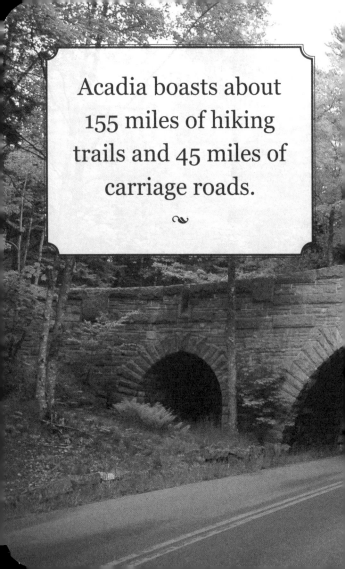

Acadia boasts about 155 miles of hiking trails and 45 miles of carriage roads.

I have become totally enamored of

everything the place has to offer:

the park, the woods, the moss, the sea, the granite cliffs and outcroppings, the ponds, the climate, the views, the other islands, the abundant seafood, and the diverse outdoor activities.

—Martha Stewart (*Food + Wine,* August 13, 2017)

Cairn at the summit of Beehive Trail.

May we leave, eventually,
as we all must—after
a long weekend
or a brief fifty years—
with this place inside us—
or rather, with this place
firmly inside itself.

—Christian Barter, Acadia's first Poet Laureate, from "The Venture"
(2016)

I will now tell anyone that along a beautiful coast, full of many beautiful spots to stop and enjoy the landscape, Acadia is among the most beautiful. And as the face Maine shows the world, it is a bright one.

—Alexander Chee, "Acadia National Park: Maine's Bright Face" (*The New York Times*, June 30, 2016)

Over 2 million people visit Acadia each year.

∾

Park visitors await sunrise on the summit of Cadillac Mountain.

About Cider Mill Press
Book Publishers

Good ideas ripen with time. From seed to harvest,
Cider Mill Press brings fine reading, information,
and entertainment together between the covers
of its creatively crafted books. Our Cider Mill
bears fruit twice a year, publishing a new crop
of titles each spring and fall.

BOOK
PUBLISHERS

"Where Good Books Are Ready for Press"

Visit us on the Web at
www.cidermillpress.com
or write to us at
PO Box 454
12 Spring St.
Kennebunkport, Maine 04046